KU-049-902

J.Davifon_ pinx.

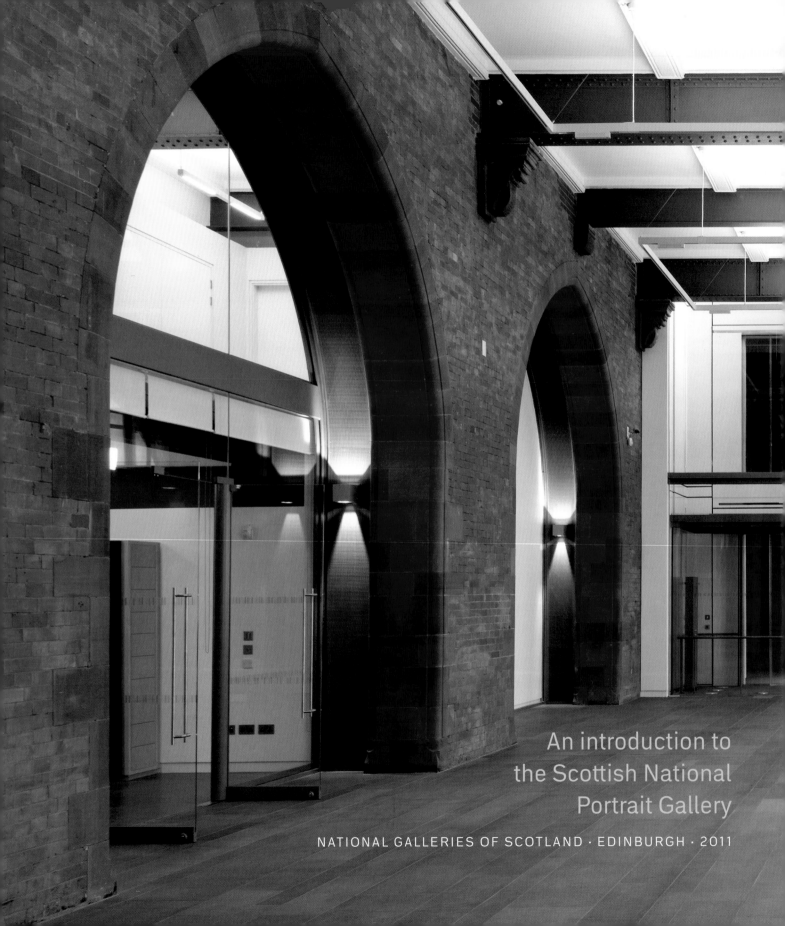

An introduction to
the Scottish National
Portrait Gallery

NATIONAL GALLERIES OF SCOTLAND · EDINBURGH · 2011

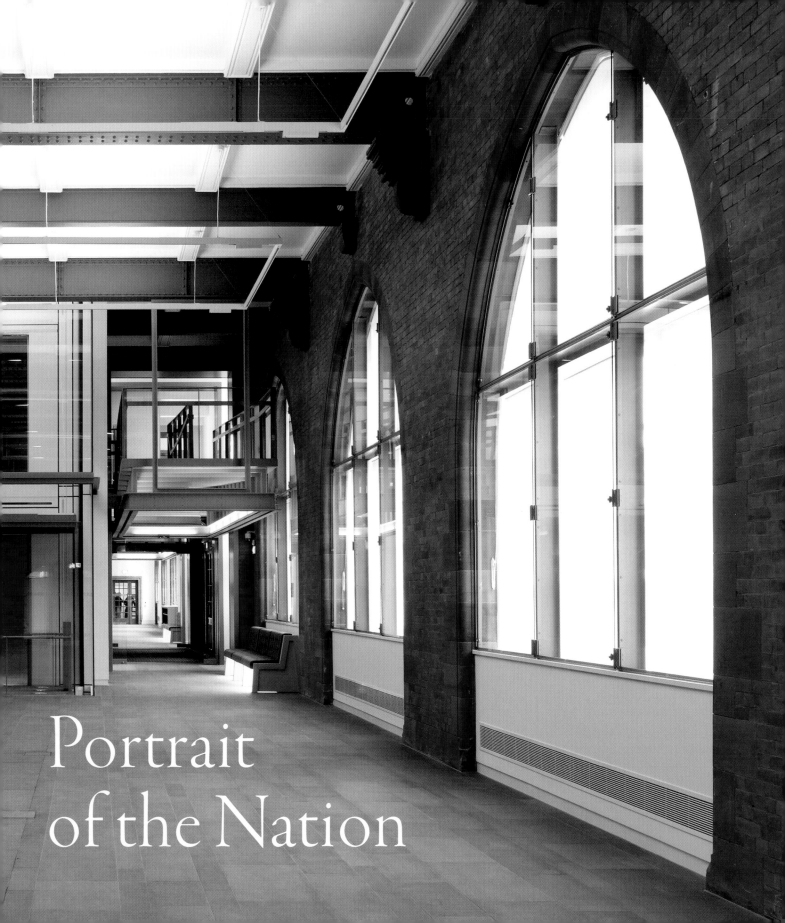

Portrait of the Nation

Published by the Trustees of the National Galleries of Scotland 2011

Text © the Trustees of the National Galleries of Scotland
ISBN 978 1 906270 37 7

Front cover: *Esther Kello (1571–1624)* by an unknown artist, 1595

Page 1: *James Douglas, 14th Earl of Morton (1702–1768) and his Family*
by Jeremiah Davison, 1740 [detail]

Pages 2 & 3: the ground floor of the renovated Gallery

Back cover: *Mr Laing or Laine* by Robert Adamson
and David Octavius Hill, 1843

Designed by Dalrymple
Typeset in Garamond Premier and Embarcadero
Printed on Chromomat 150gsm
by Die Keure, Belgium

The proceeds from the sale of this book go towards supporting the
National Galleries of Scotland. For a complete list of current publications,
please write to: NGS Publishing at the Scottish National Gallery of
Modern Art One, 75 Belford Road, Edinburgh EH4 3DR
or visit our website: www.nationalgalleries.org

National Galleries of Scotland is a charity registered in Scotland
(no.SC003728)

Scottish National Portrait Gallery renewal supported by

Foreword

The foundation of the Scottish National Portrait Gallery in 1882 was a remarkable act of faith: faith in the power of portraits to inspire and instruct, and faith that the tiny nucleus of a collection would one day expand to encompass the whole gamut of Scottish talent and achievement. Our reopening in December 2011 vindicates the vision of those far-sighted men and women of Victorian Scotland who championed the Portrait Gallery and raised the money needed to create a great building. It acknowledges too the efforts of the people of our time who have contributed in many different ways to the renaissance of the Gallery.

This book celebrates this recent renovation and introduces the new presentation of the now extensive and outstanding collection. It marks what quite rightly can be considered the coming of age of the Scottish National Portrait Gallery, now one of Scotland's most cherished institutions. We are extremely proud of the Portrait Gallery and grateful to everyone who has supported its renewal; in particular we wish to acknowledge the generosity of the Scottish Government, the Heritage Lottery Fund and The Monument Trust alongside the many other funds, trusts and donors who contributed to this great project.

JOHN LEIGHTON
Director-General, National Galleries of Scotland

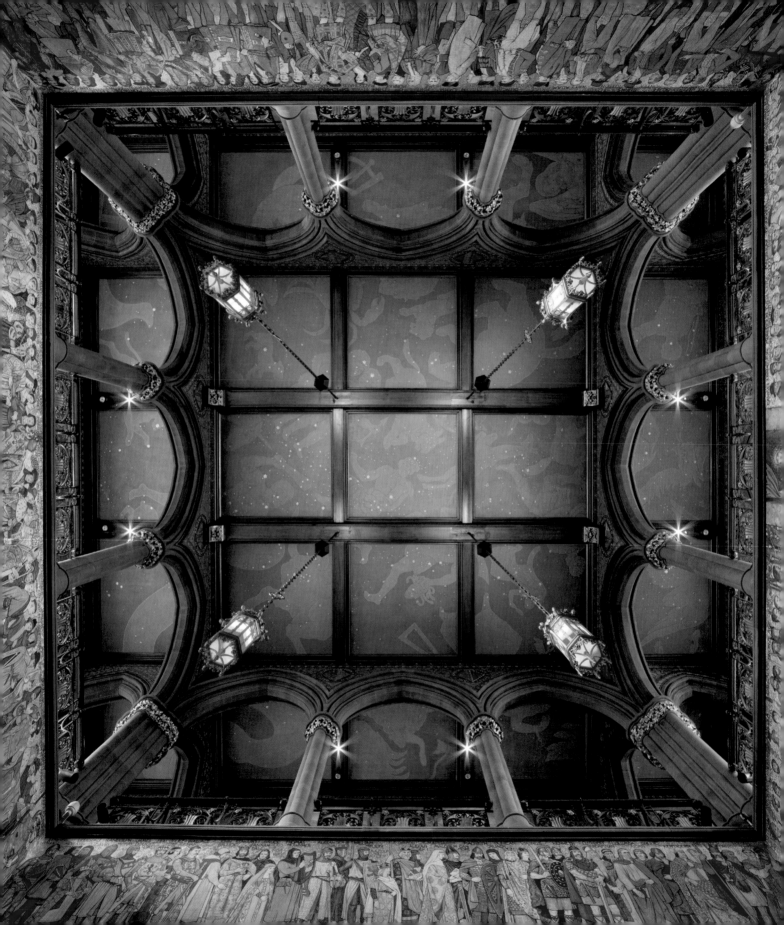

Welcome
to the Scottish National Portrait Gallery

This Gallery is about the people of Scotland – past and present, famous or forgotten. The portraits are windows into their lives and the displays throughout the building help explain how the men and women of earlier times made Scotland the country it is today. This book will introduce you to some of our country's greatest individuals and help steer you through Scotland's quite complicated but always fascinating history. There is much to see, and, most importantly, to enjoy.

Let me begin by taking you back in time to the last years of the nineteenth century, when Queen Victoria reigned over a British Empire that spread across the globe. This was when the Gallery was newly-built. The people who created the Scottish National Portrait Gallery in the 1880s believed that the study of portraits of great people would inspire visitors, including future generations. But, without the vision and deep pockets of newspaper magnate John Ritchie Findlay, the Scottish National Portrait Gallery would have remained a dream. He championed the project and paid the bills. He worked very closely with his architect Sir Robert Rowand Anderson, who created a dramatic masterpiece which resonates with Scotland's history while providing beautiful spaces in which to display the collection.

If Findlay or Rowand Anderson were able to come back today, they would find the Great Hall, with its colourful murals and marble statues, looking as good as it did in their day. They would climb the same stairs and encounter many of the great portraits which were proudly on show at the close of the nineteenth century.

And yet this book marks the most substantial renovation in the Gallery's history and there are many things that the two Victorians would be surprised to see. The first is the new glass lift that takes you up to the top floor. Another is the space set aside for Education. There was no café in the nineteenth century (nor for most of the twentieth century, for that matter), nor was there originally a shop, an information point or a lecture room. What have been introduced in the last three years by our architects Page\Park are the modern facilities that a present-day visitor expects in a great public institution. But, as well as providing these, the renovation has also restored Rowand Anderson's masterpiece to the way he originally wanted it to look. If you visited the Gallery before 2009, the year we closed for work to start, you may remember the building as being dark and the layout of rooms confusing. This was because over the years windows had been blocked and ceilings lowered. The windows are now revealed and ceiling heights have been restored so natural light floods the building. Rooms which had been offices or stores have been returned to galleries. Also, until 2009, the building was shared with the Royal Museum of Scotland which meant that the Gallery only occupied a little over half the space. With the removal of the museum to Chambers Street and substantial financial backing from the Scottish Government, the Heritage Lottery Fund and many other organisations and

← The frieze of figures from Scottish history beneath the painted ceiling of the Great Hall in the Scottish National Portrait Gallery

individuals, John Ritchie Findlay and Rowand Anderson's wish for the whole to be dedicated to the illustration of Scottish history has finally come true.

Long before the contractors moved on site in November 2009 the Gallery's curators and education staff were planning a new interpretative strategy reflecting the richness and breadth of the collections and the exciting potential of the new spaces. A decision was taken that the displays should reflect the wide-ranging nature of the collections and that there should be an increased emphasis on landscape, Scottish art, and photography. The relationship of the Scottish people to their rural and urban environments is central to the story of Scotland itself. The Gallery already had a very interesting collection of painted and photographic views of the country but loans from our sister galleries, the Scottish National Gallery and the Scottish National Gallery of Modern Art, and from the National Library of Scotland have helped strengthen this considerably. Portraiture was the main expression of art in Scotland until the early nineteenth century so it made sense to play to this strength, and place Scottish art at the forefront of our visitors' experience. In our opening exhibitions a number of individual artists are featured in depth: George Jamesone, Allan Ramsay, Thomas Annan and John Lavery. The Gallery's outstanding collection of photography was also an asset to be exploited. We will be showing much more than we were able to in the past and screening film and video, something that we rarely did before.

This guide has five sections which relate to five key periods in Scottish history. They were chosen as times when Scotland had her strongest connections with the wider world. The earliest is **Reformation**, the most recent **Contemporary**. In between, chronologically, are **Enlightenment**, **Empire** and **Modernity**. This is how the new Portrait Gallery is now laid out. Within each of these broad periods, you will find several exhibitions. For instance, in **Modernity** there is one substantial show, **War at Sea**, which looks at Scotland's contribution to the Allied naval victory in the First World War. A smaller display, **The Modern Scot**, examines the cultural renaissance of the mid-twentieth century in which the poet Hugh MacDiarmid was such a towering figure, whilst another, **Pioneers of Science**, celebrates Scotland's remarkable recent record of medical and scientific discovery. This guide will give you a taste of all seventeen exhibitions spread over the three floors of the building.

On the top floor are nine galleries which examine aspects of Scotland from about 1540 to the end of the nineteenth century, covering **Reformation**, **Enlightenment** and **Empire**. As well as some substantial historical exhibitions – on the Jacobites or the Scottish Enlightenment, for instance – there are smaller displays on Highland dress and Glasgow's slums. Moving downstairs to the middle floor, don't miss the new Photography Gallery which is the first dedicated space for photography exhibitions in the National Galleries of Scotland. The opening show, **Romantic Camera**, where almost every work comes from our own world-class collection, is not to be missed, nor is the adjacent library. This wonderful wood-panelled room was originally the library of the Society of Antiquaries of Scotland and, unless you were a member of that exclusive institution, inaccessible. As part of the renovation the library was taken down, timber by timber, moved from the top to the middle floor and from the east to the west side and reassembled. It will now perform a range of functions, traditional and new. This is where the Gallery's collection of works on paper (prints, drawings and photographs) can be seen. It is also where our great archive of portraits of Scots in collections all over the world can be consulted. But you don't need to be a scholar or make an appointment to enjoy the library. Examine some of the handsome portrait medallions by James Tassie or view the exquisite portrait miniatures or, if you are so minded, reflect on the plaster casts of the heads of Scotland's most infamous murderers.

Passing from the western side of the building, you will walk across the upper level of the Great Hall on the Ambulatory, another great space to view the Victorian architecture and decorations. This is the ideal spot to admire the murals around you, recently cleaned in time for the reopening. Scotland's great victories like Bannockburn and Stirling Bridge are celebrated here in paintings by William Hole. This is not the place for defeats. Look up and you can enjoy the starry sky, freshly revealed after the painstaking removal of decades of soot and dirt. Look down a little to see the frieze, a painted pageant of great Scottish individuals from the Victorian philosopher and campaigner for portrait galleries, Thomas Carlyle, back to the Stone Age via Flora Macdonald and Macbeth. The Ambulatory is also where you can engage with **Faces and Places**, our digital exploration of the collection.

Moving to the east side of the building you will find the exhibitions in the **Modernity** section. In addition, the room at the far end is showing a specially-commissioned display, **Migration Stories: Pakistan** which profiles high-achieving individuals drawn from Scotland's Pakistani community. The **Contemporary** section, on the ground floor, is the world of today. Here you will find photographs of celebrities as well as the major exhibition **Missing**, a video installation specially commissioned from Graham Fagen for our reopening. Findlay and Rowand Anderson's Gallery was concerned solely with the famous, but this work, a project made in association with the National Theatre of Scotland, looks at people, often unknown, who have disappeared – the flip side to the great and the good of the traditional portrait gallery.

In the months ahead some exhibitions will change and be replaced by others and over the next five years the entire Gallery will be re-hung. That doesn't mean that Mary, Queen of Scots and Robert Burns will disappear, merely that the contexts in which they are shown will change.

I hope you enjoy your visit. The staff of the Portrait Gallery, and of the National Galleries of Scotland of which we are part, look forward to welcoming you back.

JAMES HOLLOWAY
Director, Scottish National Portrait Gallery

The Building

The Scottish National Portrait Gallery was designed by Sir Robert Rowand Anderson in the 1880s to be a shrine to the nation's history and its people's achievements. Even without its great collection of portraits, this building would still be a unique and powerful representation of Scotland, a unified vision which comprises the statues of notable figures on the façade, the colourful murals of significant Scottish events and the pageant frieze of Scottish worthies in the Great Hall. Rowand Anderson also understood that the growing collection would take up the later story of Scotland, so the decoration of the building, inside and out, concentrates on the earlier part of the nation's history, up to the mid-sixteenth century when portraiture first took root in Scotland.

**The Entrance to the Scottish
National Portrait Gallery**
by Adam Alexander Inglis ←

albumen print, photographed in 1895

Sir William Wallace (about 1274–1305)
by William Birnie Rhind ↙

sandstone, sculpted about 1891–3

Wallace's victories against the English
established an independent Scotland. In 1297
he won the decisive battle of Stirling Bridge
over the army of King Edward I, but he was
later captured and taken to London where
he suffered a gruesome death. Much of our
knowledge about William Wallace comes from
the fifteenth-century poet, Blind Harry.

The Good Deeds of King David I
by William Hole ←

on the wall of the Balcony, painted in 1901

William Hole shows King David with the
Abbey of Holyrood, founded in 1128, under
construction and the king giving orders for
further religious buildings. Reform of ecclesi-
astical institutions and the revival of religion
were passions that David (about 1085–1153)
was able implement during his reign.

Macbeth (about 1005–1057)
and **Queen Margaret** (died 1093)
by William Hole ↑

from the frieze in the Great Hall,
painted in 1898

It was the English playwright Shakespeare
who made Macbeth the most famous of all
Scottish kings in his great tragedy written
for another Scottish ruler, James VI and I.
In reality, Mac Bethad mac Findlaích, as he
was known, was described by near contemporaries as 'Mac Bethad the renowned' and
'the generous king'. He was the only reigning
Scottish monarch to make a pilgrimage
to Rome.

Queen Margaret arrived in Scotland as
a refugee. A member of the royal house of
Wessex, she fled England after William the
Conqueror became king. Scotland's only royal
saint, Margaret, who married King Malcolm
III, founded Dunfermline Abbey. Queensferry
on the Forth is named after her.

Reformation

Reformation is the earliest of the sections which structure our displays and it charts the introduction and development of portraiture in Scotland from the mid-1500s to the end of the seventeenth century. The Scottish nation underwent seismic changes in this period. Protestantism became the official religion after centuries of Catholicism, and in 1603 the royal court moved south to London after King James VI inherited the English throne. Scots began to commission artists, often major continental figures, to record their likenesses and these images played a significant role in the struggles for power, identity and nationhood.

The major exhibition **Reformation to Revolution** considers these themes and includes iconic characters from Scottish history. **George Jamesone: Scotland's First Portrait Painter** looks at this celebrated native-born artist whilst **John Slezer: A Survey of Scotland** explores the earliest published views of the nation's towns, buildings and countryside.

← Detail from a portrait of Mary, Queen of Scots (1542–1587)

Mary, Queen of Scots (1542–1587)
by an unknown artist after François Clouet ↑

oil on panel, probably nineteenth century

Mary, Queen of Scots was sent to France as a child for her safekeeping. Raised at court, she later married the heir to the French throne. This portrait shows her aged eighteen, in the white mourning dress of the French court after the death of her husband, François II in 1560. Soon after the original of this portrait was painted, Mary returned to Scotland, a Catholic monarch in a newly Protestant nation.

PG 186 bought in 1887

Mary, Queen of Scots (1542–1587)
by an unknown artist ←

oil on canvas, painted about 1610–15

After returning from France, Mary ruled in Scotland for only six years. Following a rebellion, she fled to England. She was held captive for nearly twenty years before being executed for plotting to murder her cousin, Queen Elizabeth I. Painted over twenty years after her death, this portrait aimed to restore Mary's reputation. The crucifix shows the biblical story of Susanna and the Elders, in which an innocent woman was saved from being put to death.

PG 1073 bought in 1925

IOANNES CNOXVS.

John Knox (1505–1572) ↑
by an unknown artist, after Adrian Vanson

woodcut, made in 1580

John Knox was the religious leader of the
Protestant Reformation in Scotland. A militant
Calvinist, he composed the Confession of
Faith which was adopted by the parliament

of 1560 as the basis of the new Scottish Kirk.
Knox's numerous pamphlets include his
notorious *First Blast of the Trumpet against
the Monstrous Regiment of Women*. He
famously clashed with Mary, Queen of Scots.
PGE 27 bequeathed by William Findlay
Watson in 1886

James Hepburn, 4th Earl of Bothwell
(about 1535–1578)
by an unknown artist ←

oil on copper, painted in 1566

Bothwell became infamous as the third
husband of Mary, Queen of Scots. He married
her in 1567, three months after the murder of
her second husband, Lord Darnley, despite
being acquitted of this crime only the month
before. PG 869 bought in 1917

James Douglas, 4th Earl of Morton
(about 1516–1581)
by Arnold Bronckorst ↑

oil on panel, painted about 1580

Morton was one of the Protestant Lords
who destabilised the reign of Mary, Queen
of Scots. He was the last regent of Scotland
during James VI's minority, and brought a
period of peace and stability to the kingdom.
In this portrait, Morton is shown with a view of
Tantallon Castle, his East Lothian stronghold,
in the background.
PG 1857 bought in 1959

Esther Kello (1571–1624)
by an unknown artist ←

oil on panel, painted in 1595

The artist Esther Kello was a Protestant Frenchwoman whose family had fled religious persecution, eventually settling in Edinburgh. During her career she produced a large number of calligraphies and manuscripts, as well as miniatures and embroideries. Kello received commissions from the Stuart royal family, Queen Elizabeth I and various aristocrats.

PG 3556 gifted by the Society of Antiquaries of Scotland in 2009

Tom Derry
by Marcus Gheeraerts the Younger →

oil on canvas, painted in 1614

Tom Derry was Anne of Denmark's fool or jester, employed to provide entertainment at her court. A so-called 'natural fool', that is, born with learning difficulties, Derry became a much-loved and prominent member of the queen's household. He had servants of his own and he moved to London with Anne in 1603.

PG 1111 bequeathed by A.W. Inglis in 1929

James VI and I (1566–1625)
attributed to Adrian Vanson ←→

oil on panel, painted in 1595

James VI did not like having his portrait painted and here we sense his weariness at having to sit for an artist. James is wearing expensive clothes, appropriate to his royal status, with a doublet embroidered in gold thread and an ermine-lined cloak. The jewelled 'A' and 'H' on his hat represent his wife, Anne of Denmark, and Prince Henry, the heir she had produced the year before.

PG 156 bought in 1886

James VI and I (1566–1625)
by Nicholas Hilliard ←

watercolour on vellum, painted about 1609

The celebrated artist Nicholas Hilliard painted all the members of the Scottish royal family after they arrived in England in 1603. This miniature is still in its original gold case, decorated with blue and white enamelling, which complements the colour scheme of the portrait.

PGL 153 on long-term loan in 2001

Charles I, when Duke of York and Albany (1600–1649)
by Robert Peake ←

oil on canvas,
painted about 1610

The future Charles I was
the second son of James VI
and I and his queen, Anne
of Denmark. The young
prince has been painted in
a luxurious setting and he
is wearing an expensive
costume embroidered with
silver thread and shoes
with huge rosettes. The
stuffed bird-of-paradise on
his hat, which came from
New Guinea, was an exotic
decoration that emphasises
Charles's elite status.

PG 2212 bequeathed by the
13th Lord Elibank in 1973

Falkland Palace and the Howe of Fife
by Alexander Keirincx ←

oil on panel,
painted about 1639

Falkland Palace in Fife was a royal hunting lodge, and a favourite home of the Scottish kings and queens. James V built the Renaissance building we see in Keirincx's painting with its distinctive gate-house towers, although the east range of the palace is now ruined and the fenced deer park no longer exists. Charles I commissioned this painting, probably because he stayed at the palace during his visit to Scotland in 1633.

PG 2409 bought in 1977

Seton Palace and the Firth of Forth
by Alexander Keirincx ←

oil on panel,
painted about 1639

This painting and the view of Falkland Palace by Keirincx are the earliest landscape paintings of Scotland. Seton Palace was one of the grandest Renaissance palaces in the kingdom. It was the home of the Earl of Winton, a childhood friend of Charles I. The king stayed there twice, with his court, during his visit to Scotland in 1633.

PG 2696 bought in 1986

George Jamesone
Scotland's First Portrait Painter

George Jamesone (1589/90–1644) was the first great Scottish-born artist in a profession dominated by foreigners. Born in Aberdeen, Jamesone served his apprenticeship in Edinburgh as a painter of decorative interiors. He returned to Aberdeen and set up a studio, working as a portrait painter. His sitters included aristocrats, merchants, lawyers and academics, and he was commissioned to produce a series of Scottish monarchs for King Charles I's official entry into Edinburgh in 1633. Jamesone became very wealthy but, despite his great success, the political and religious upheavals of the time affected him – he was arrested and briefly imprisoned in 1639.

Lady Anne Erskine, Countess of Rothes (?–1640), and her daughters, Lady Margaret Leslie (1621–1688) and Lady Mary Leslie (1620–?) by George Jamesone →

oil on canvas, painted in 1626

This fascinating picture is an early example of a Scottish noble family using portraiture for display and dynastic advancement. The sitters are depicted wearing their finest clothes and jewels. They stand in a grand room, presumably representing their country seat, Leslie House, in Fife. The room includes elements of an aristocratic Scottish interior, with a timber ceiling, leaded windows with a coat-of-arms, and a collection of portraits by Jamesone.

PG 2456 bought in 1980

George Jamesone (1589/90–1644)
by George Jamesone →

oil on canvas, painted about 1642

Jamesone's intriguing self-portrait is one
of his most striking works. Jamesone
presents himself primarily as an artist
– he holds a palette and brushes in one
hand, and points at a wall of pictures,
which includes various portraits,
presumably painted by him. The fact that
Jamesone portrays himself dressed as a
gentleman is significant, indicating that
his work has brought him social status
and financial success.

PG 2361 bought in 1976

Campbell of Glenorchy Family Tree
by George Jamesone ←

oil on canvas, painted in 1635

In 1635 Sir Colin Campbell of Glenorchy
asked Jamesone to paint a family tree. Like
many of his contemporaries, Glenorchy
was fascinated by genealogy, especially by
the history of his own family. Jamesone's
picture uses the format of the Tree of
Jesse, a familiar motif to contemporary
viewers, from the biblical Book of Isaiah.
Glenorchy's ancestor, Duncan Campbell of
Lochawe, reclines at the foot of the cherry
tree. [detail]

PG 2167 bought in 1968

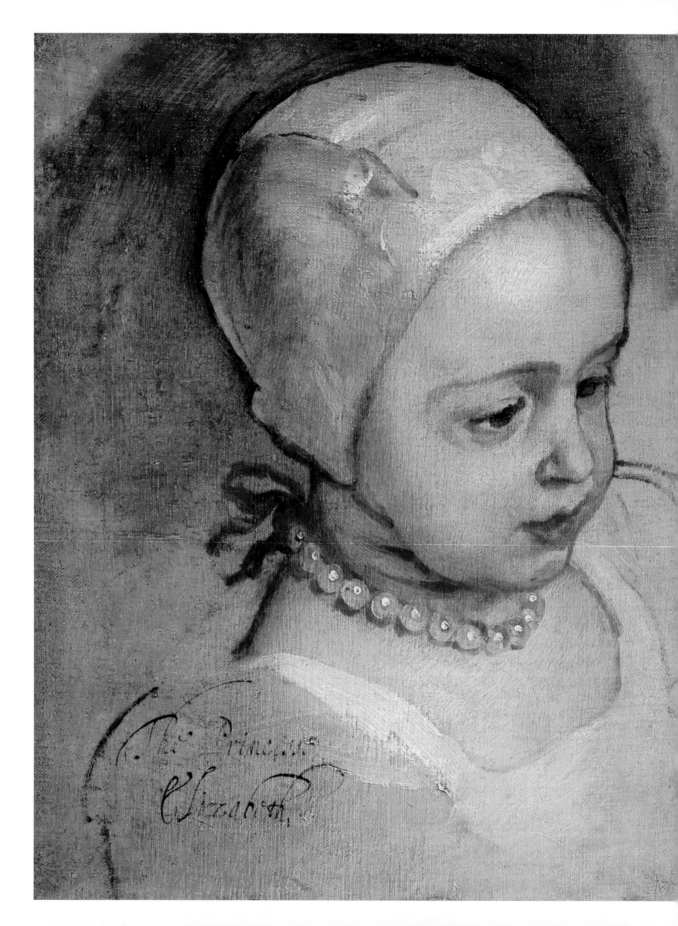

Princess Elizabeth (1635–1650)
and **Princess Anne** (1637–1640)
by Sir Anthony van Dyck

oil on canvas, painted in 1637

This touching depiction of Princesses
Elizabeth and Anne is a sketch for
a group portrait of the five children
of Charles I and Queen Henrietta
Maria, commissioned by the king
from Van Dyck in 1637. This is the only
preparatory sketch painted from life
that the celebrated Flemish artist
produced in England.

PG 3010 bought with the assistance
of the Heritage Lottery Fund, the
Scottish Office and the Art Fund in
1996

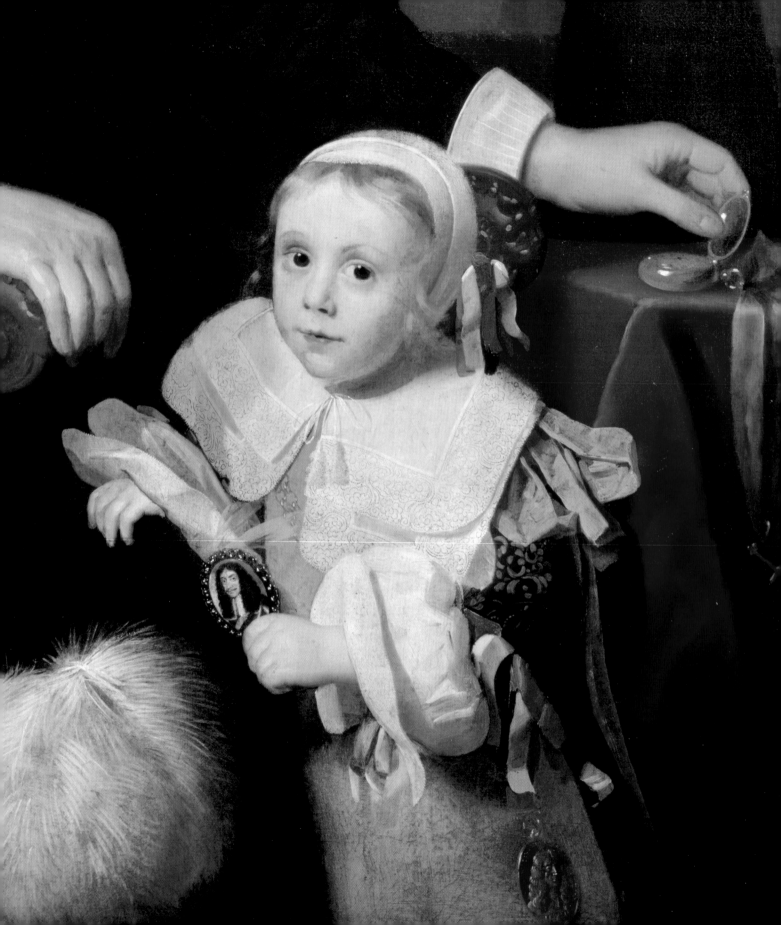

Sir William Davidson of Curriehill
(about 1615–1689) **and his son Charles**
(about 1662–1666) ← →
by Abraham Lamberstz van den Tempel

oil on canvas, painted about 1664

Davidson was a Scottish merchant based in
Holland. He supplied money and information
to the exiled king, Charles II. Davidson's
son was added to the portrait at a later date,
possibly after his death in 1666. He was
Charles II's godson, and he holds a miniature
of the king.

PG 2462 bought in 1980

The King's Departure from
Scheveningen 1660
by Pieter van Abeele ↓

silver, made in 1660

This medal was struck to commemorate
Charles II leaving the Netherlands for
England at the Restoration. In Van den
Tempel's portrait one of these medals can be
seen hanging from a ribbon on the child's arm.

PG 751 bought in 1910

Queen Anne, when Princess of Denmark (1665–1714) by Willem Wissing and Jan van der Vaart ←→

oil on canvas, painted about 1685

Queen Anne, the second surviving child of James VII and II and his first wife, Anne Hyde, was the last member of the House of Stuart to reign. The roses and her left hand pointing towards her stomach allude to Anne as mother of hoped-for heirs. No children survived to adulthood from Anne's eighteen pregnancies and her Protestant cousin inherited the throne as George I, the first Hanoverian monarch of Great Britain.

PG 939 bought in 1922

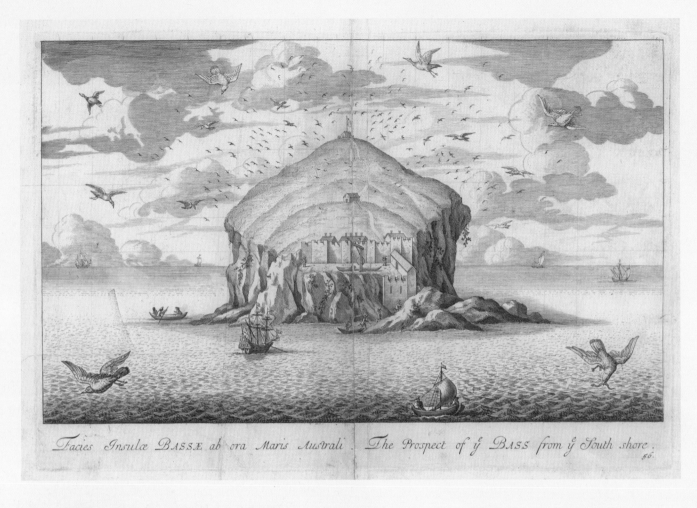

Facies Insulæ BASSÆ ab ora Maris Australi. The Prospect of ỹ BASS from ỹ South shore.

John Slezer A Survey of Scotland

John Slezer was a military surveyor, employed by the Scottish army to assess the nation's defences and fortifications. He produced images of many of the places he visited, publishing them as engravings in 1693 in a book called *Theatrum Scotiae* (*A Theatre of Scotland*). His printed images are the earliest published views of the nation's towns, buildings and countryside and presented a comprehensive view of Scotland for the first time.

The Bass Rock
after John Slezer ↑

engraving, made before 1693

This engraving of the Bass Rock, a volcanic plug in the Firth of Forth, is one of Slezer's best-known images. The island's castle, sited at the top of the cliffs, was used as a jail, and many Scots were imprisoned there during the religious and civil wars of the seventeenth century. In 1691, two years before the print was published, the rock was captured and held by the Jacobites.

National Library of Scotland

Edinburgh – The North-East View of Edinburgh Castle (detail)
after John Slezer →

engraving, made before 1693

Born in Germany or the Low Countries, John Slezer arrived in Scotland in 1669 and Edinburgh became his adopted home. He knew the Castle well: as Chief Engineer, he had drawn up proposals to upgrade the defences.

National Library of Scotland

Enlightenment

The Enlightenment of the eighteenth century was a European phenomenon in which Scotland played a leading role. Many ideas that we now take for granted – in economics, sociology and the sciences, for example – were first proposed in the universities, societies and salons of Edinburgh and Glasgow. David Hume, the great philosopher and historian, and his friend the artist Allan Ramsay are the subject of **Citizens of the World**, one of the major exhibitions in this section.

Hume and Ramsay were committed to the reigning House of Hanover but many Scots, known as Jacobites, supported the return of the exiled Stuart dynasty. The exhibition **Imagining Power** looks at their campaigns – in politics, pictures, and on the battlefield.

Tartan was associated by the British government with Jacobites and subversive politics and it was banned as everyday wear in 1747. **Blazing with Crimson**, a display looking at some Scots who chose to be depicted in Highland dress, demonstrates how the meaning of tartan shifted according to sitter and time.

← Detail from the portrait of John Hope, 2nd Earl of Hopetoun (1704–1781)

Allan Ramsay (1713–1784)
by Michael Foye ←

marble, sculpted in 1775–77

Like many Enlightenment figures, the artist Allan Ramsay was fascinated by antiquity and he undertook four extended visits to Italy. This bust was sculpted in Rome during his third trip. After a fall from a ladder in 1773, Ramsay was no longer able to paint, so he spent his time in Italy searching for the site of the Latin poet Horace's country villa.

PG 641 bought in 1905

Anne Ramsay née Bayne (died 1743)
by Allan Ramsay →

oil on canvas, painted about 1739

Anne Bayne was the artist's first wife and this portrait dates from around the time of their marriage. The highly finished surface, with all evidence of brushwork smoothed away, illustrates well the contemporary view that Ramsay's paintings were 'rather lick't than pencill'd'. Anne died giving birth to their third child.

PG 2603 bought in 1983

David Hume (1711–1776)
by Allan Ramsay →

oil on canvas, painted in 1754

Ramsay painted this the year he co-founded the Edinburgh Select Society, a debating club which met weekly. The philosopher David Hume was one of the original members. Topics for discussion included the treatment of women in ancient and modern societies, paper credit, and poor relief, but the most contentious issues of the day – religion and Jacobitism – were off the agenda. Ramsay painted his friend in informal dress, wearing a soft velvet cap to keep his shaven head warm.

PG 3521 accepted by HM Government in Lieu of Inheritance Tax and transferred to the Scottish National Portrait Gallery in 2008

Adam Ferguson (1723–1816)
by Sir Joshua Reynolds ↓

oil on canvas, painted in 1781–82

Ferguson was one of the major figures of the Scottish Enlightenment. A professor of philosophy at the University of Edinburgh, his activities also included diplomacy (he negotiated with the Americans at Philadelphia), farming (implementing agricultural improvements) and the church (as a young army chaplain, he denounced the Jacobites, France and Catholicism). Considered a pioneer of sociology, his writings were admired by Voltaire and influenced Hegel and Marx.

PG 2890 bought in 1992

Adam Smith (1723–1790)
by James Tassie ↘

paste medallion, made in 1787

The philosopher David Hume had a profound influence on his friend, Adam Smith. Like Hume, Smith saw his work as contributing to a 'science of man' which would establish a better understanding of modern society.

His *Inquiry into the Nature and Causes of the Wealth of Nations*, published in 1776, remains the seminal manifesto of early free market capitalism. Unlike Hume, however, Smith was a rather private man who was happiest in the company of his mother in Kirkcaldy.

PG 157 bought in 1886

Robert Adam (1728–1792)
by James Tassie →

paste medallion, made in 1792

Architect Robert Adam evolved and made fashionable the elegant neoclassical townhouses and palatial country houses of the later eighteenth century. Combining first-hand knowledge of the antique with his distinctive and delicate sense of the visual, Adam created a complete stylistic language, embracing interior decoration and furniture. Tassie's medallion, which imitates an antique cameo profile, was made at Adam's death, although it depicts the architect as a young man. [detail]

PG 2590 bought in 1983

James Douglas, 14th Earl of Morton
(1702–1768) and his Family
by Jeremiah Davison ←

oil on canvas, painted in 1740

Like many Scottish aristocrats at this
time, Morton played an active role in the
pursuit of scientific knowledge for practical
improvement. One of the founders of the
Philosophical Society of Edinburgh, he
became President of the Royal Society in
London and a member of the Académie
Royale des Sciences in Paris. This portrait
shows the earl, his first wife, Agatha, and
their children.

PG 2233 bought in 1974

John Hope, 2nd Earl of Hopetoun
(1704–1781)
by Allan Ramsay →

oil on canvas, painted in 1748

This portrait was commissioned by the
Royal Infirmary of Edinburgh in 1745 to
honour their most important benefactor, the
2nd Earl of Hopetoun. Ramsay presented
the finished work to the recently-founded
hospital as a gift, knowing that it would
be seen there by the leading lights of
Edinburgh society. Formal in pose and dress
– the earl wears the ermine-trimmed robes
of a peer of the realm – this is a dignified
representation of a public-spirited man.

PGL 1430 on long-term loan from the Royal
Infirmary of Edinburgh in 2004

James Francis Edward Stuart, Prince of Wales (1688–1766)
by Nicolas de Largillière ↑

oil on canvas, painted in 1691

This chubby toddler, shown with his loyal spaniel, was the son of James VII and II. His birth, in June 1688, precipitated a revolution in the British Isles. That autumn Prince William of Orange, a Dutch Protestant, invaded England, and King James fled to France with his family. Supporters of the exiled dynasty were now known as 'Jacobites', a term which comes from the Latin form of James.

PG 2191 bought in 1971

The Battle of Glenshiel, 10 June 1719
by Peter Tillemans →

oil on canvas, painted in 1719

For nearly 100 years Jacobitism was a major factor in European affairs and it was responsible for the last battles on British soil. The 1745 Rising is the best known of the Jacobites' bids to restore the Stuart monarchy, but there were several other attempts. The 1719 Rising ended with the Jacobites' defeat at Glenshiel in the Highlands. This painting is based on eye-witness accounts of the battle.

PG 2635 bought with the assistance of the National Heritage Memorial Fund and the Art Fund in 1984

James III congratulating his son, Prince Henry Benedict, on the occasion of his elevation to Cardinal York, July 1747
by Paolo Monaldi, Pubalacci and 'Silvestri'

oil on canvas, painted in 1747–48

In July 1747 Prince Henry, the younger brother of Bonnie Prince Charlie, became a cardinal in the Roman Catholic church. This large painting shows him receiving his father's congratulations in front of their palace in Rome, lavishly decorated for the occasion. Prince Charles was furious as he, like many Jacobites, felt that this closer association with Roman Catholicism would make a Stuart restoration still more difficult.

PG 3269 bought with the assistance of the Heritage Lottery Fund and the Art Fund in 2001

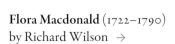

'A Likeness notwithstanding the Disguise'
by Richard Cooper ←

hand-coloured etching, made in 1745

This print advertises the massive reward of £30,000 offered by the British government in August 1745 for the capture of Prince Charles Edward Stuart, who had landed in the Outer Hebrides in late July. The prince is referred to dismissively as 'the Son of the Pretender'. However, Cooper's fanciful figure is not a real likeness of Charles, it is based on an earlier engraving of a soldier who had been executed for mutiny in 1743.

SP IV 123.49 provenance unknown

Flora Macdonald (1722–1790)
by Richard Wilson →

oil on canvas, painted in 1747

Flora Macdonald famously helped Prince Charles evade capture in the aftermath of the Jacobite defeat at Culloden in April 1746. With the prince disguised as her maid, they reached Skye in a small boat just as the government militia were closing in. The prince escaped, but Flora was arrested and taken to London. This portrait was painted for a young naval officer on the ship which took Flora south.

PG 1162 bought in 1931

Prince Charles Edward Stuart
(1720–1788)
attributed to William Mosman ←

oil on canvas, painted about 1750

Before the momentous events of 1745, Prince Charles had only worn Highland dress as fancy dress to masquerade parties in Rome. Once in Scotland, leading the last and most famous of the Jacobite Risings, he wore it regularly, aware of its symbolic power and capacity to inspire loyalty amongst his men.
PG 1510 bequeathed by Miss F.D. Robertson in 1948

Prince Charles Stewart
by Ozias Humphrey →

black chalk on paper, drawn in 1776

This drawing shows Prince Charles towards the end of his life when he was living in Florence as the 'Count of Albany'. No longer the vigorous hero of the 1745 Rising, Charles's health was now poor – he suffered from dropsy, digestive problems, alcoholism and asthma. Nevertheless, British visitors on the Grand Tour were fascinated to catch a glimpse of the man who had been the 'Young Pretender'. [detail]
PG 2991 bought with the assistance of the Patrons of the National Galleries of Scotland in 1995

Blazing with Crimson
Tartan Portraits

Highland dress and tartan fabric have become universally recognised signs of Scotland and Scottish identity. With its focus on five grand full-length portraits, this display explores what Highland dress meant to different people at different times. At first associated specifically with the elite warrior culture of the Gaelic north and west of the nation, the tartan plaid and kilt signified high fashion as well as pride in Scottish ancestry. Highland dress was later adopted by the army and the kilted soldier became a powerful symbol of the wider British Empire. Smaller pictures, including the first photographs of tartanclad sitters, take the story into the nineteenth century, when British kings and queens led an obsession with Highland costume.

Major James Fraser of Castle Leathers (1670–1760)
attributed to John Vanderbank ↙

oil on canvas, painted about 1720

Major James Fraser wears a tartan coat, plaid and trews (*triubhas*). There are two different patterns or setts – the simple check of the trews and coat, and a bolder design for the plaid or mantle. It was fashionable to wear a mix of tartans, the brighter the better. During the 1715 Jacobite Rising Fraser served with government forces. This assertive portrait conveys Fraser's ease with weaponry and pride in his Highland identity.

PGL 276 on loan from a private collection

Kenneth Sutherland, 3rd Lord Duffus (died 1734)
by Richard Waitt ↓

oil on canvas, painted about 1712

Wearing a belted plaid of red, black and yellow tartan, and a fancy waistcoat slashed to reveal fine linen beneath, Lord Duffus is pictured as an idealised Gaelic aristocrat, the *sealgair sithne* or 'hunter of deer'. His dress conveys the wealth implied by this, but his estates in Moray gave a poor living. Exiled after the 1715 Jacobite Rising, Duffus became an officer in the Imperial Russian Navy, only returning to his homeland shortly before his death.

PG 1095 bought in 1928

Crimean Heroes
by Joseph Cundall ↑

albumen print, photographed in 1856

William Noble, Alexander Dawson and John
Harper fought in the Crimean War with the
72nd Highlanders. They were photographed
on their return at the request of Queen
Victoria, wearing the uniform in which they
had gone into battle.

PGP 140.7 bought in 1992

**John Campbell, later 3rd Earl of
Breadalbane** (1696–1782)
by Charles Jervas ←

oil on canvas, painted in 1708

The status of this charming child as heir to
one of the great Highland families is underlined by his stylish costume and the imaginary
mountainous landscape before which he
stands. The complex pattern of the boy's
tartan belted plaid or great kilt (*feileadh mor*)
is set off by the bright blue slashed doublet.

PG 2934 bought with the assistance of the
National Heritage Memorial Fund and the
Art Fund in 1993

Empire

The union of Scotland and England in 1707 led to new opportunities for Scottish merchants and investors. Glasgow boomed on the transatlantic trade in sugar and tobacco. Great Britain's growing military power and expanding empire created openings for ambitious Scots across the world. International trade, as well as developments in industry and farming, brought unparalleled wealth to Scotland. The exhibition **Age of Improvement** looks at some of the people who drove these changes.

Greater leisure encouraged widespread participation in sport and this is explored in the other main exhibition in this section, **Playing for Scotland**. It was during this period that Scotland's population became predominantly urban. But, with the expansion of Scottish cities, came over-crowding and disease. Thomas Annan recorded some of Glasgow's worst slums before their demolition; his photographs can be seen in **Close Encounters**. **Out of the Shadow** looks at the opportunities available to women in the nineteenth century which, compared to men, were few.

← Detail from the portrait of William Forbes of Callendar (1756–1823)

A View of Stornoway
by James Barret

oil on canvas, painted in 1798

The bustling harbour of Stornoway, the
largest port in the Western Isles, is a vision
of a successful community where fishing
and farming have brought prosperity to the
people. This was partly true. While Barret's
view, painted for the Mackenzie family who
owned much of Lewis, shows herring fishing,
kippering and maritime trade, the cattle and
sheep in the foreground are a reminder that
these incomers had begun to displace the
local population, leading to emigration.

PG 3291 bought in 2002

Robert Burns (1759–1796)
by Alexander Nasmyth ↙

oil on canvas, painted in 1787

Scotland's national bard was painted by his friend Alexander Nasmyth soon after Burns had his first great taste of success with the publication in Kilmarnock of *Poems, Chiefly in the Scottish Dialect.* This portrait was painted to be engraved as the frontispiece for the Edinburgh edition of the poems. While he was in the capital, Burns met many of the great men and women of Enlightenment Scotland including James Hutton and the young Walter Scott.

PG 1063 bequeathed by Colonel William Burns in 1872

Sir Walter Scott (1771–1832)
by Sir Henry Raeburn →

oil on canvas, painted in 1822

It is difficult to overestimate the popularity and influence of Sir Walter Scott in his time. Originally trained as a lawyer, he made a fortune from his writing. Scott's poetry, including works such as *The Lay of the Last Minstrel* and *The Lady of the Lake,* and his novels, *Waverley* and *Rob Roy* for example, explored Scotland's turbulent history.

PG 1286 bought with the assistance of the Art Fund in 1935

Sir David Wilkie (1785–1841)
by Sir David Wilkie ←

oil on canvas, painted about 1804–5

This is probably the last picture that Wilkie
painted before settling in London. He had
already made his mark in Scotland with
scenes of rural life in his native Fife. He
quickly established himself in the south as
one of the most brilliant and innovative artists
of his time. In this accomplished self-portrait
the young artist, aged only twenty, stares
searchingly out at us.

PG 573 presented by J. Rankin in 1898

Sir Henry Raeburn (1756–1823)
by Thomas Campbell →

marble, sculpted in 1822

Henry Raeburn was the leading portrait
painter in Scotland at the beginning of the
nineteenth century. It is through his portraits
that we can picture the men and women who
dominated Scottish society at this period. A
remarkable feature of this sculpture is that
Raeburn did not sit to Campbell – the sculptor
captured Raeburn's likeness by using engravings after the painter's self-portrait.

PG 1037 bought in 1926

James 'Purlie' Wilson (1757–1820)
by an unknown artist ↓

oil on panel, painted about 1810

This modest portrait depicts James Wilson, a weaver from Strathaven in Lanarkshire who became famous as one of the 'Radical Martyrs'. Unemployment and economic depression prompted a group of men to plan an armed uprising. The government arrested eighty-eight radicals and tried them for high treason. The majority of the men found guilty were transported to Australia, but Wilson was publicly hanged on Glasgow Green.

PG 3361 bought in 2003

Sir Alexander Morison (1779–1866)
by Richard Dadd →

oil on canvas, painted in 1852

The artist Richard Dadd suffered from psychotic delusions. He murdered his father and was imprisoned in a mental hospital in London. Sir Alexander Morison, his physician, encouraged Dadd to continue painting. In the background of this portrait is Anchorfield, the doctor's house on the Firth of Forth, which Dadd copied from drawings sent by a member of Morison's family.

PG 2623 bought with the assistance of the National Heritage Memorial Fund in 1984

James Hutton (1726–1797)
by Sir Henry Raeburn ←

oil on canvas, painted about 1776

James Hutton was one of the
founders of modern geology.
Raeburn refers to Hutton's
interests by showing geological
specimens beside the manuscript
for his highly influential paper
Theory of the Earth. The *Theory*
concluded 'we find no vestige of a
beginning, no prospect of an end',
challenging the orthodox belief
that earth had been created by God
about six thousand years earlier.

PG 2686 bought with the assistance of the National Heritage
Memorial Fund and the Art Fund
in 1986

William Forbes of Callendar
(1756–1823)
by Sir Henry Raeburn →

oil on canvas, painted in 1798

William Forbes was a self-made
man. The son of an Aberdeen
merchant he began work as a
coppersmith and won a government contract to sheathe ships'
hulls in copper. This process
prolonged the time a ship could
remain out of port and was there-
fore of great benefit to the British
navy. With his new fortune Forbes
bought the estate of Callander
near Falkirk and commissioned
Scotland's leading artist to paint
this grand portrait.

PGL 327 on long-term loan
in 1984

Romantic Camera

The Scottish National Portrait Gallery has the best collection of photography in Scotland and our renovated building now has a gallery devoted to photographic exhibitions. The first exhibition in this new space, *Romantic Camera*, contains many of the great masterpieces of the collection, which range from the very earliest years of the medium to the present day. *Romantic Camera* explores the relationship between romanticism and photography in Scotland and shows how the camera, a mechanical instrument, helped to create a nostalgic vision of a place and a people.

The Queen, Balmoral, 1863.
G. W. Wilson   Aberdeen

Queen Victoria on Fyvie with John Brown at Balmoral
by George Washington Wilson ←
albumen carte de visite, photographed in 1863

Washington Wilson was the most successful British commercial photographer of his era. This photograph was originally conceived by Queen Victoria as a tribute to her late husband, Prince Albert. In its first year of publication, this and a few similar images, sold almost 13,000 copies, their popularity doubtless heightened, ironically, by the rumour-mongers who referred to the Queen as 'Mrs Brown'.
PGP R 884 presented by Mrs Ann Riddell in 1985

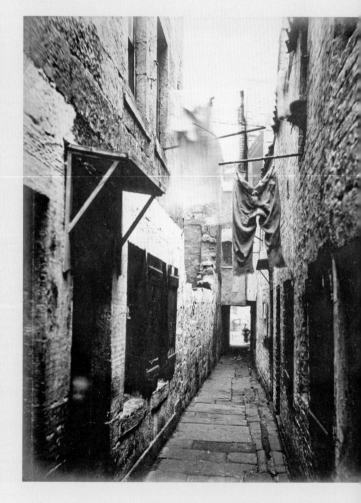

Thomas Carlyle (1795–1881)
by Julia Margaret Cameron ← ←

albumen print, photographed in 1867

In 1843 the Scottish sage, Thomas Carlyle, published *Past and Present*, the most articulate mid-century expression of romantic principles. The book contrasted a modern world degraded by machines and money to the fulfilment offered by a medieval monastic community. *Past and Present* had a profound influence on Victorian society.

PGP 373.1 bought in 2007

Close No 46 Saltmarket
by Thomas Annan ←

albumen print, photographed in 1868–71

Thomas Annan began his series of thirty-one photographs of the closes and wynds of old Glasgow in 1868. This area was one of the worst urban slums in Britain and had recently been scheduled for demolition by the city. The series is acknowledged as the first record of slum housing in the history of photography.

PGP 185.10 bought in 1986

St Kilda
by Alexander Hutchison ↑

albumen print, photographed about 1890

Hutchison's image of St Kilda – the desolate archipelago forty miles west of the Outer Hebrides – reveals an encounter between the impoverished islanders and visitors from the mainland. Doubtless Hutchison arrived on one of the summer steamers that then visited the island and this photograph was probably intended as a souvenir of his meeting with a community that Victorians celebrated as 'primitive'.

PGP 172.2 presented by the National Monuments Record in 1990

Catherine Waterston (née Sandeman) (1755–1831)
by George Simson →

oil on canvas, painted in 1822

Catherine Sandeman married an Edinburgh merchant who dealt in sealing wax, candles and torches. When her husband died in 1780, Catherine decided to continue running the business. Two years after his death, she opened a shop on Edinburgh's Lawnmarket, where, in addition to wax products, she sold 'Juniper's Patent Essence of Peppermint', a popular cure-all for everything from stomach complaints and hangovers to seasickness.

PG 3331 gifted by Miss Leonora Waterston in 2003

Anne Grant of Laggan (née MacVicar) (1755–1838)
by Augustin Edouart ↘

cut paper, made in 1831

Anne MacVicar married the parish minister of Laggan in Inverness-shire. When she was widowed she supported herself and her eight children by writing. Her first book, *Letters from the Mountains*, was published in 1806. Her reputation was established by the time she moved to Edinburgh in 1810. Anne became a friend of Sir Walter Scott, and it was she who first guessed that he was the author of *Waverley*.

PG 1177 bought in 1932

Isabella Smith (née Ewing) of Jordanhill (1755–1855)
by James Graham Gilbert →

oil on canvas, date unknown

Isabella Ewing's husband Archibald Smith made his fortune in the West Indies. Jordanhill was their home in Renfrew, near Glasgow. Her friend, the writer Mrs Grant of Laggan, was prompted by this portrait to recall Isabella's 'gentle mind' and her 'modest mental charms untaught to shine'.

PG 3646 gifted by Mrs Babington-Smith in 2009

Mrs Elizabeth Johnstone Hall ↑
Jeanie Wilson and Annie Liston ↗
by Robert Adamson and David Octavius Hill

carbon prints made in 1916 (from negatives made 1843–46)

The port of Newhaven, two miles north of the centre of Edinburgh, was the subject of a series of photographs made by the pioneer photographers Adamson and Hill. Newhaven fishwives would walk into town every day carrying one to two hundredweight of fish in creels to sell. The fishwives were noted for their striking appearance and independent spirit.

PGP HA 358 & PGP HA 359 provenance unknown

Phoebe Anna Traquair (née Moss) (1852–1936)
by Peter Induni →
after James Pittendrigh Macgillivray

marble, sculpted in 1927

Phoebe Traquair was a distinguished illuminator, embroiderer and enameller. She painted murals for St Mary's Cathedral Song School and the Catholic Apostolic Church in Edinburgh. This bust depicts her in working smock and cap as the artist craftswoman.

PG 1463 transferred from the Scottish Modern Arts Association in 1944

Playing for Scotland

Modern sport has its origins in the nineteenth century when migration from the countryside to cities, together with increased leisure time and the advent of the railways, encouraged mass participation. *Playing for Scotland: the Making of Modern Sport* explores the transformation of sport during this period.

At the beginning of the 1800s sport was enjoyed as an irregular and local activity. This tradition was overtaken during the century as newly-formed national sports bodies in Britain introduced sporting codes with standardised rules. The first national sporting society in Scotland was the Royal Caledonian Curling Club. By the outbreak of the First World War the parameters of sport had expanded with a wider choice of sports and increased opportunities to play.

Dr Nathaniel Spens of Craigsanquhar (1728–1815)
by Sir Henry Raeburn →

oil on canvas, painted in 1793

Dr Nathaniel Spens wears the shooting uniform of an honorary officer of the Royal Company of Archers. The Royal Company was the first sporting society to be established in Scotland and from 1822 became the official bodyguard to the monarch during royal visits to Scotland. By 1840 there were around twelve other archery clubs and the sport was 'practised as an elegant and pleasant pastime by ladies and gentlemen'. On loan from the Queen's Bodyguard for Scotland (Royal Company of Archers)

William, John and Eliza Middleton playing Croquet
by William Crawford ←

oil on canvas, painted in 1864

The eldest daughter of the merchant John Middleton plays croquet with two of her younger brothers. Croquet was a popular game with the prosperous classes. Formal competitive croquet began in 1870 when the first Scottish Croquet Championship was held; the Scottish Croquet Club was founded five years later.

PG 3518 gifted by Mr and Mrs Tremaine Arkley in 2007

Mr Laing or Laine
by Robert Adamson and David Octavius Hill ←←

calotype, photographed in 1843

Real tennis was the forerunner of lawn tennis and had been played in Scotland since the sixteenth century. Photography was in its infancy when this image was taken. Because of the lengthy exposure time, struts positioned at the back of the tennis player support him, and his racket may be held up with string.

PGP HA 558 provenance unknown

Scotland Rugby Team
by an unknown photographer ←

albumen print, photographed in 1877

The first rugby international was played between Scotland and England. Two years later the Scottish Rugby Union was founded. Scotland fielded a team of fifteen players for the first time in their match against Ireland in 1877. This photograph shows the Scottish rugby team which won against England the following month. The captain, R. W. 'Bulldog' Irvine (seated third from the left in the middle row), was renowned as a 'destructive' tackler.

PGP 393.3 bought in 2008

Modernity

The twentieth century brought changes to Scotland as fundamental as any in the past. Britain had entered the century with Victoria still queen and an empire unrivalled by any country in history. Glasgow and the industrial cities made goods for the world which were carried on ships built in the great yards of the Clyde. By the end of the century Scotland had lost its manufacturing base and Britain its empire. In *War at Sea* Sir John Lavery, one of the Glasgow Boys, recorded Scotland's part in Britain's titanic struggle with Germany for naval supremacy in the First World War. This culminated in 1918 with the surrender of the German fleet on the Firth of Forth, within sight of this Gallery. *Pioneers of Science* celebrates Scottish scientists and their inventions and discoveries, while *The Modern Scot* explores the cultural nationalism of the poet Hugh MacDiarmid and his circle, which offered and celebrated a distinctively Scottish voice.

← Detail from a portrait of Naomi Mitchison, Lady Mitchison (1897–1999)

A Convoy, North Sea, from N.S.7
by Sir John Lavery →

oil on canvas, painted in 1918

Lavery was a successful portrait painter when he was commissioned by the War Office to record the First World War at sea. He chose his own itinerary and subject matter, visiting naval ports, shipyards, airfields and munitions factories in Scotland and on the southern coasts of England.

On loan from the Imperial War Museum

Scapa Flow, Orkney, from the Signal Station
by Sir John Lavery ↘

oil on canvas, painted in 1917–18

Orkney comprises a large number of islands, many of which are located around Scapa Flow, one of the biggest natural harbours in the world and the base for the British Grand Fleet in the First World War. The German High Seas Fleet was interned in the channel known as Bring Deeps after the Armistice in November 1918.

On loan from the Imperial War Museum

James Maxton (1885–1946)
by Sir John Lavery ←

oil on panel, painted about 1933

James Maxton strongly opposed the First World War. He was imprisoned in 1916 after a speech on Glasgow Green in which he encouraged munitions workers to strike. He entered parliament at the 1922 General Election as the Labour MP for Glasgow Bridgeton. Maxton became a good friend of John Lavery; artist and politician were golfing companions.

PG 1416 bequeathed by the artist in 1941

Packing Ropes for the Navy in an Unidentified Factory
by George P. Lewis ↓

photograph taken in 1917 or 1918, printed by Peter Cattrell in 2004

The war brought more than one and a half million women into employment, replacing the work of men who were serving in the armed forces. This photograph shows four people, three of whom are women, working in the ropewalk at a rope factory, possibly the Gourock Ropeworks Company in Port Glasgow.

PGP 310.18 commissioned by the Scottish National Portrait Gallery in 2004 from a negative held by the Imperial War Museum

Poets' Pub
by Alexander Moffat ↑

oil on canvas, painted in 1980

A group of celebrated poets forms a constellation around the figure of Hugh MacDiarmid, the leader of the Scottish Renaissance Movement and one of the most influential writers of the twentieth century. The setting is a composite of Edinburgh's literary pubs: the Café Royal, Milne's Bar and the Abbotsford. The painting celebrates the legacy of the Scottish Renaissance Movement of the inter-war years and Bohemian Edinburgh in the 1950s and 1960s.

PG 2597 bought in 1983

Francis George Scott (1880–1958)
by William Johnstone ↗

oil on canvas, painted in 1933

This painting identifies the composer with his native Borders landscape and the Eildon Hills in particular. Scott was a Modernist who drew on tradition, setting words by Robert Burns and finding inspiration in folk music.

PG 2849 bought in 1991

Willa Muir (née Anderson)(1890–1970)
by Nigel McIsaac ↗

oil on plywood, painted in 1944

Willa Muir, writer and translator, is also known as the wife and partner of the writer Edwin Muir, whom she married in 1919. During the early 1920s, the couple travelled extensively in

Europe working as teachers and translators. Their Kafka translations made the Czech author's work available to the English-speaking public.

PG 2186 gifted by the artist in 1970

Fionn MacColla (Thomas Douglas Macdonald) (1906–1975) by Edward Baird ↑

oil on gesso, painted in 1932

Fionn MacColla was the pen name of the writer Thomas Macdonald. In 1928, MacColla and the artist Edward Baird joined the newly-founded National Party of Scotland. This painting was exhibited as a *Portrait of a Young Scotsman*. Baird wrote that it was his 'attempt to paint a modern and distinctively Scottish portrait'.

PG 3669 bought in 2011

Naomi Mitchison, Lady Mitchison (1897–1999) by Wyndham Lewis ←

oil on canvas, painted in 1938

Naomi Mitchison is shown frowning because, as she said later, she just wanted to get on and complete *The Blood of the Martyrs*, one of her many novels. Lady Mitchison was a campaigner for many liberal causes, spending nearly twenty years as a local councillor in Argyll. Towards the end of her long life she became the Mabakgatla, or mother, of the Bakgatla tribe in Botswana.

PG 3351 bought with the assistance of the Patrons of the National Galleries of Scotland and the Art Fund in 2003

Robert Louis Stevenson (1850–1894)
by Count Girolamo Nerli ↑

oil on canvas, painted in 1892

This portrait was painted on Samoa where
R.L. Stevenson, the author of *Treasure
Island* and *Kidnapped*, had been living for
three years. The artist, Count Nerli, has
caught the writer's look of tiredness and
strain, the effects of a lifetime of ill-health.
The darker side of Stevenson's imagination is revealed in his novel *The Strange
Case of Dr Jekyll and Mr Hyde*.
PG 847 bequeathed by Mrs Turnbull
in 1915

Sir James Matthew Barrie (1860–1937)
by Sir William Nicholson ↑

oil on canvas, painted in 1904

This portrait was painted when the artist was
working on the sets for the first stage adaptation
of Barrie's novel *Peter Pan*. Before the opening
night many of Barrie's friends voiced their misgiv-
ings about the extraordinary story and the special
effects which they thought would be impossible
to stage. But Barrie went ahead, confident not
only that it would succeed but that it would
become a regular Christmas entertainment.
PG 1438 bought with the assistance of the Art
Fund in 1943

Charles Rennie Mackintosh (1868–1928)
by Francis Henry Newbery →

oil on canvas, painted in 1914

In 1894 Mackintosh, who had recently
graduated from Glasgow School of Art, was
commissioned to design new premises for
the school in Renfrew Street. He owed this
remarkable commission to the imagination
of the director, Fra Newbery. It is now acknowledged as one of the supreme buildings
of the twentieth century and Mackintosh
is recognised as one of Europe's greatest
architects and designers.
PG 1205 bought in 1933

Joseph Crawhall (1861–1913)
by E.A. Walton ↓

oil on canvas, painted in 1884

Crawhall and Walton were two leading members of a group of artists known as the Glasgow Boys. They were inspired by contemporary French painting. Walton's practice of manipulating thick paint with square-ended brushes and a palette knife is typical of the technique of the Glasgow Boys in their prime in the 1880s.

PG 971 gifted by the artist's widow in 1924

Pioneers of Science

Scotland has an impressive tradition of producing pioneers of science, medicine and technology; it also has a well-deserved reputation as a centre for scientific innovation. *Pioneers of Science* showcases people whose theories, experiments, discoveries and inventions have helped shape the modern world and whose legacy continues to influence and inspire developments in the twenty-first century. The term 'scientist' was first commonly used in the late nineteenth century to describe those who investigated the natural world through experiments performed according to scientific methods. In 1883, the Scottish mathematician and physicist, Lord Kelvin underlined the importance of science for everyday life: 'the life and soul of science is its practical application'.

Dr John Scott Haldane (1860–1936)
by an unknown photographer ↓

silver gelatine print, photographed about 1906

John Scott Haldane researched the mechanics of breathing. In extreme conditions such as sewers, mountaintops and mines (in which he was the first to introduce canaries to test for poisonous gases) he tested his theories by experimenting on himself. In this photograph Haldane poses in his diving equipment. His experiments for the British Admiralty were carried out in top secret – the presence of the German soldier alongside him is a mystery.

PGP 160.1 gifted by the family of the late Mrs John Scott Haldane in 1962

Sir Ronald Ross (1857–1932)
by Gurupada Chitrakar ↑

vegetable dyes fixed with vegetable gum on paper, painted in 2010

This scroll depicts Sir Ronald Ross discovering how malaria was spread. Whilst working for the Indian Medical Service in 1898, Ross found it was the *Anopheles* mosquito which carried the malaria parasite and spread the disease. He was awarded the Nobel Prize in Physiology or Medicine in 1902.

Gurupada is a storyteller and picture-maker (chitrakar) from Bengal. He paints narrative scrolls and sings their stories as they unroll. [detail]

SNPG Library 31. Ros. Chi bought in 2010

Anaesthetist John Bracken and Farm research assistant Douglas McGavin at The Roslin Institute
by Wendy McMurdo →

laserchrome prints, photographed in 2002

This is one of a set of four photographs of staff at The Roslin Institute of the University of Edinburgh, an international centre for research on the molecular and quantitative genetics of farm animals. The people in this series are all key members of the team that created Dolly the sheep, the first mammal cloned from an adult cell.

PGP 299.3 commissioned by the Scottish National Portrait Gallery in 2002

James Clerk Maxwell (1831–1879)
by Alexander Stoddart →

bronze, cast in 2009

This is a model for the statue of James Clerk Maxwell in Edinburgh's George Street. With his dog Toby at his feet, Clerk Maxwell holds a spinning colour top. This device enabled him to analyse the phenomenon of colour perception. His theory of electromagnetism influenced Einstein, who remarked that his predecessor's theories were 'the most profound and the most fruitful that physics has experienced since the time of Newton'.

PG 3658 gifted by Walter and Norma Nimmo in 2010

Three Oncologists
by Ken Currie → →

oil on canvas, painted in 2002

The artist Ken Currie has captured the anxiety associated with cancer in this powerful triple portrait of three oncologists. As pioneering cancer specialists they are depicted as ready, able and prepared to fight and destroy the dreaded disease.

When this portrait was painted Professor Robert Steele (left), Professor Sir Alfred Cuschieri (centre) and Professor Sir David Lane (right) were members of the Department of Surgery and Molecular Oncology at Ninewells Hospital and Medical School in Dundee.

PG 3296 commissioned by the Scottish National Portrait Gallery in 2001

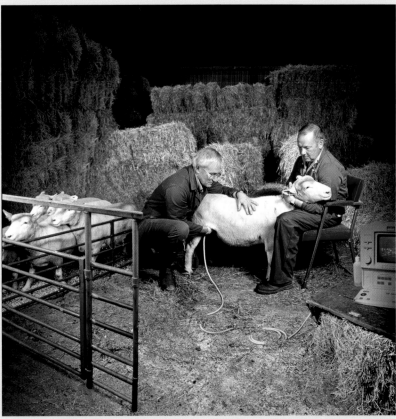

Aerial View of Edinburgh
by Alfred Buckham ←

silver gelatine print, photographed
about 1920

Buckham's career as a photographer was
transformed by the First World War when
he entered the Royal Naval Air Service
as an instructor. The techniques of aerial
reconnaissance were evolving rapidly and
by 1918 photographs could be taken from as
high as 18,000 feet. Buckham's prints reveal
extensive manipulation, often exposing two
or more negatives in order to capture the
immensity of land and cloudscape.

PGP 197.1 bought in 1990

Untitled from the series
'The Family of Miners'
by Milton Rogovin →

silver gelatine print, photographed in 1982

The American photographer, Milton Rogovin,
arrived in Scotland in 1982 and captured the
miners at a crucial moment in their history,
just before the strikes and closures that
would devastate Scotland's mining communities. Rogovin's concern was to record the
figure of the miner, at work and at leisure, as
straightforwardly as possible.

PGP 371.2 presented by the photographer
in 2006

Children, the Gorbals, Glasgow
by Roger Mayne →

silver gelatine print, photographed in 1958

Mayne, the most sophisticated street photographer in Britain during the immediate
post-war period, used his camera to investi-
gate the potential of the urban environment
as a site of social renewal. He was especially
fascinated by the utopian nature of childhood play.

PGP 193.5 bought in 1993

Dame Muriel Spark (Muriel Sarah
Camberg) (1918–2006)
by Alexander Moffat ←

oil on canvas, painted in 1984

As a child at school in Edinburgh, Muriel
Spark and her classmates fell under the spell
of a remarkable teacher, Christina Kay. As
Spark wrote later, Miss Kay was a character
in search of an author. The resulting novel
was *The Prime of Miss Jean Brodie* written, of
course, by Spark herself.
PG 2617 commissioned by the Scottish
National Portrait Gallery in 1984

Baroness Kennedy – Helena I,
(Helena Kennedy) (born in 1950)
by Glenys Barton →

ceramic, made in 1997

Helena Kennedy QC is one of Britain's leading
lawyers and a Labour member of the House
of Lords. In this low-relief ceramic bust,
the Baroness raises her hand in a dramatic
gesture.
PG 3395 bought in 2004

Contemporary

We cannot see our own age with the hindsight of history. But we can attempt to make judgements about the significance of current events and mark those issues that we think will define our time.

Modern mass communication has led to the cult of the celebrity. **Hot Scots** picks a number of talented younger men and women who maintain their fame by an astute manipulation of their image. In contrast **Missing**, a specially commissioned video piece by Graham Fagen, explores those who have disappeared and who only become known to us, if at all, by virtue of their absence.

Global migration has established itself as one of the key issues of the twenty-first century. The emigration of Scots across the world is by no means a recent phenomenon. Likewise, people from elsewhere have settled in Scotland since earliest times. **Migration Stories: Pakistan** looks at the relatively new Pakistani community in Scotland through the lens of German photographer Verena Jaekel.

← Detail from a portrait of Karen Gillan

Untitled
from the series 'The Brave Ones'
by Zwelethu Mthethwa ↓

digital C-type print, photographed in 2010

This image depicts two South African boys from the Shembe Nazareth Baptist community, a denomination that blends Christian and Zulu traditions. Its young male adherents refer to themselves as the 'Iscotch' and adopt special costumes based on the kilt for religious ceremonies. The influence is drawn from Scottish regiments present in Natal in the late nineteenth century.

PGP 778 bought with the assistance of the Art Fund in 2011

Landscape, 7/004
by Michael Reisch ↘

digital C-type print,
photographed in 2007

Using the latest modelling software, the German photographer, Michael Reisch, transforms familiar landscapes, in this case Glencoe, into teasing, imaginary terrains. With all signs of human habitation removed – no sheep, fences, houses, or roads – his photographs take on a utopian, even primordial dimension.

PGP 382.4 commissioned by the Scottish National Portrait Gallery in 2007

Billy Connolly (born in 1942)
by John Bellany ↓

oil on canvas, date unknown

'The Big Yin' (The Big One), as Billy Connolly is known, served an apprenticeship as a welder in the Clyde shipyards before embarking on a career in show business. He initially focused on folk singing but gradually made the transition to stand-up comedy and acting.

PG 3378 presented by the artist in 2004

John Byrne (born 1940)
by John Byrne →

oil on blockboard, painted 1971–73

John Byrne, playwright, theatre designer and artist, grew up in Paisley. He used his experience working as a paint-mixer in a carpet factory there to create his play *The Slab Boys*. He designed the sets for one of the most celebrated Scottish plays of the post-war years, John McGrath's *The Cheviot, The Stag and The Black, Black Oil* and wrote the cult television series *Tutti Frutti* in the 1980s.

PG 3068 presented by the Scottish Arts Council in 1997

Kenny Dalglish
(born in 1951)
by Mark I'Anson →

mixed media on paper, made
in 2003

Kenny Dalglish is widely
regarded as the most
successful British footballer
of his generation. Born in
Glasgow, Dalglish grew up
supporting Rangers, but
it was their great rivals,
Celtic, who signed him in
1967. Ten years later he
moved to Liverpool where
he played for the team that
won the European Cup three
times. In May 2011 Liverpool
announced that Dalglish
had been given a three-year
contract as manager.
PG 3343 commissioned
by the Scottish National
Portrait Gallery in 2003

The Castlemilk Lads
by Oscar Marzaroli ↑

silver gelatine print, photographed in 1963

This photograph was shot on one of the sprawling peripheral housing estates thrown up rapidly in Glasgow during the 1950s. It speaks of dislocation, of a city and its working-class communities transformed beyond all recognition by town planners. The extraordinary posture and expression of the two central figures encourage us to speculate about the boys' relationship to the ill-defined environment in which they now stand.

PGP 101.3 bought in 1985

Port Glasgow Town Hall Christmas Party
by Mark Neville →

digital C-type print, photographed in 2004

In 2004 Mark Neville spent a year as artist-in-residence in Port Glasgow producing a photographic book which he then distributed free as gifts to the community. This image, featuring Betty Robertson, appeared on the front cover and quickly assumed an iconic status. It revealed, in the words of another resident, that 'we like a good party'.

PGP 420.1 bought in 2008

Karen Gillan (born 1987)
by Suki Dhanda

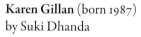

digital C-type print, photographed in 2010

Karen Gillan is most famous for the role
of Amy Pond in *Doctor Who*. She grew up
in Inverness and at the age of sixteen she
enrolled at Telford College in Edinburgh and
then transferred to acting school in London.

PGP 791 bought in 2011

The Weight
by Jack Vettriano

oil on canvas, painted in 2009

This self-portrait shows one of Britain's favourite artists. Born Jack
Hoggan in 1951 and brought up at Methil in Fife, Vettriano is self-taught.
He first came to attention exhibiting at the Royal Scottish Academy in
1988, after which his career took off. This painting was donated by him
to an auction in aid of the Terence Higgins Trust. It was inspired by a
photograph taken by Fredi Marcarini at the artist's home in London.

PGL 2385 on long-term loan from a private collection in 2011

Aamer, Ifet and Qais Mir Anwar
by Verena Jaekel

digital C-type print, photographed in 2011

Born in England, Aamer Anwar moved to Scotland to study mechanical
engineering at the University of Glasgow and became a political activist.
He was the Scottish organiser for the Anti-Nazi League and worked for the
Commission for Racial Equality, before going to law school. He qualified as
a solicitor and now runs his own company. In this photograph Anwar and his
wife wear the costume they wore for their wedding.

PGP 779.1 commissioned by the Scottish National Portrait Gallery in 2011

Roy Dennis (born in 1940)
by Alison Kinnaird ←

engraved crystal glass, made in 2003

Roy Dennis is best known for his work on the conservation of rare birds and the reintroduction of species such as the white-tailed eagle and osprey. The red kite, another successfully reintroduced breed, appears in various modes of flight throughout this portrait.

PG 3330 commissioned by the Scottish National Portrait Gallery in 2003

Susan Boyle (born in 1961)
by John Swannell →

archival digital print, photographed in 2010

In April 2009 Susan Boyle from West Lothian appeared as a contestant on *Britain's Got Talent*. She became an internet sensation with tens of millions of people viewing her audition, in which she sang *I Dreamed a Dream*, on Youtube. Her subsequent recording career has been phenomenal.

PGP 180.22 bought in 2011

Copyright and Photographic Credits

p.2, 3, 12 (left) © Keith Hunter photography; p.6, 96 © John McKenzie; p.13 © Antonia Reeve; p. 32, 33 © the Trustees of the National Library of Scotland; p.72, 73: © by courtesy of Felix Rosenstiel's widow & son Ltd on behalf of the estate of Sir John Lavery and by kind permission of the Imperial War Museum; p.74, 82 © Sandy Moffat; p.75 © S. Johnstone / estate of William Johnstone; © by kind permission of the Wyndham Lewis Memorial Trust (a registered charity); p.76 © Desmond Banks; p.77 © estate of Francis Henry Newbery; p.79 © Alexander Stoddart; © Wendy McMurdo; © Ken Currie; p.80 © courtesy of Richard and John Buckham; p.81 © Milton Rogovin 1982, courtesy the Rogovin Collection, LLC; p.83 © Glenys Barton, courtesy of Flowers East; p.86 courtesy of the artist and Jack Shainman Gallery, NY; p.87 © Michael Reisch, courtesy Hengesbach-Gallery, Berlin; p.88 courtesy of John Byrne / Bridgeman Art Library; courtesy John Bellany / Bridgeman Art Library; p.89 © Mark l'Anson; p.90 © Anne Marzaroli © Mark Neville; p.92 © Suki Dhanda; © Verena Jaekel; p.94 © Jack Vettriano; p.95 © John Swannell.

Mr A. D. PAGE.

11.B LUMSDEN CRESc,

ALMONDBANK,

PERTH. PH1.3LH.